# Tapestry Of The Mind

Tegh Munjral Kalra

BookLeaf Publishing

India | USA | UK

# Dedication

To my Mother and Father


Your unwavering love, endless support, and boundless wisdom have been the foundation of my life. This collection of poems is a tribute to the sacrifices you've made, the lessons you've taught, and the unconditional love you've given. Every word is a reflection of the strength, inspiration, and comfort you bring into my world.

Thank you for being my guide, my rock, and my greatest source of inspiration. This book is for you.

With all my love and gratitude,


Tegh Munjral Kalra

# Preface

Welcome to the Tapestry of the Mind,

This collection of poems is a reflection of how my vivid imagination flows through the myriad experiences of life. Each poem is a piece of my heart, capturing moments of joy, sorrow, love, and introspection.

The inspiration for these poems comes from my heart, and my strenuous training of becoming a writer. Through these verses, I aim to describe how my vivid imagination flows.

I invite you to immerse yourself in these poems, to find your own meanings and connections within them. Whether you read them in moments of solitude or share them with others, I hope they bring you as much solace and joy as they have brought me.

Thank you for joining me on this poetic journey.

With heartfelt appreciation,

Tegh Munjral Kalra.

# Acknowledgements

I would like to express my deepest gratitude to my family, friends and my mentor Mrs. Ridhhima Mohan. Your encouragement and belief in me have been invaluable.

# 1. The Disguise Within

The mask we wear,
a facade for others,
For ourselves, we show no care.

We do it just to blend in,
A disguise that hides our true kin.
It's not who we are,
yet no one sees,
The mask we wear,
full of silent pleas.

Fear grips us tight,
the fear of exclusion,
A constant pain,
a daily intrusion.

We hope our efforts aren't in vain,
As we navigate this endless strain.

# 2. Riches and Ruin

A man strolled by the river's edge,
Humble, grateful, a soul of great pledge.
He paused to reflect,
In the water's gleam,
Thankful for his simple life's serene dream.

Though wealth eluded him,
Love was his treasure,
A richness of heart,
a boundless measure.

Five years hence, the same man returned,
Corrupt, ungrateful, with bridges burned.
He gazed at his reflection,
Now wealthy yet forlorn,
His family gone, his heart deeply torn.

Riches he had, but love was lost,
He walked away, his soul tempest-tossed.

# 3. Illusion of Liberty

A man steps out, news in his stride,
Slaves like him, now free with pride.
The British gone, a new dawn's light,
Yet freedom's paradox looms in sight.

Only the rulers taste true liberty,
The rest remain in servitude's decree.
A different master, the same old plight,
In the quest for money, they lose the fight.

Freedom's illusion, a cruel jest,
Servants still, in a new conquest.

# 4. From serenity to scars

A solitary man, around forty years,
Battled depression, anxiety, and fears.
He found solace by the tranquil lake,
Where birds sang and trees would shake.

Nature's embrace healed his weary soul,
He left the city, feeling whole.
Five years later, he returned to find,
The lake's serenity left behind.

Malls and shops replaced the green,
The birds' sweet songs no longer seen.
His troubles gone, but the lake's begun,
To bear the scars of what humans have done.

# 5. Squirel chases and bacon dream.

My Playful Puppy,
George My playful puppy,
George, so dear,
On bacon he loves to gorge without fear.

He'll dash like lightning for a bone,
And curiously peek into my phone.
He waits for me with eager eyes,
Despising our garden gnome in disguise.

He's my companion, my treasured friend,
His chase with squirrels will never end.
We adore him to the very core,
In my jumper, he fits and more.

I love my dog, my loyal mate,
He devours my breakfast, never late.
I can't let him go, he's my joy,

Anyone who harms him,
I will destroy.

6

# 6. Serenity in a sip

On a cold evening or a chilled morning,
A nice cup of tea brings a warming.
The satisfaction fills my soul with glee,
A plate of jam biscuits,
a perfect spree.

Just thinking about it makes me warm,
A remedy for cold, a soothing charm.
There's a tea for every heart's desire,
To relax after a day,
to inspire.

Tea is the friend who won't depart,
A companion at sunset,
a work of art.
Hot and perfect,
it fulfills every craving,
With biscuits to dip or a scone,
so amazing.

Always there, a comforting plea,
Thank you, dear tea, for being with me.

8

# 7. A moment of serenity

A quiet morning,
peace from the world,
A tranquil dawn,
where calm is unfurled.

A cup of tea, a soothing embrace,
Relieves the soul, sets a gentle pace.
Witness the sunrise, a golden hue,Or lift weights at the
gym, feeling anew.

Play sports, away from the crowd,
Or study for exams, where silence is allowed. Finish
reading a novel,
or write one yourself,
In the stillness, find your true self.

Inner peace, as eggs and bacon sizzle,
Fulfilling your stomach, making your heart drizzle. Oh,

the joy of a quiet morning's grace,
A moment of serenity, a cherished space.

# 8. A starlit night

A starry night, a canvas of dreams,
Where darkness fades, and starlight gleams.
The moon and stars in celestial flight,
Their brilliance banishes the deepest fright.

In this serene, silent night, you find peace,
A moment where all worries cease.
The stars beckon with their gentle light,
Inviting you to marvel at their sight.

From your vantage, you indulge in the view,
A spectacle that makes everything new.
It's a time to unwind, to let go of the day,
In the embrace of the night, you find your way.

# 9. A snowball of fun

My first snowfall, a magical delight,
Transforming the world in a blanket of white.
As snowflakes kiss your skin, pure and light,
They bring a joy that feels just right.

Hot chocolate sipped by the fireside,
Snowball fights with friends, laughter worldwide.
These moments of wonder, so pure and bright,
Fill your heart with unending delight.

Building snowmen, crafting winter's art,
Each flake a masterpiece, a work of heart.
The first snowfall, a memory to hold,
A story of joy, forever retold.

# 10. A memory faded

A forgotten memory, a fleeting trace,
Of trips and faces, time can't erase.
Moments once vivid, now hard to find,
Lost in the corridors of the mind.

No names, no details, just a blurred scene,
Echoes of laughter, places we've been.
If joy was felt but now is obscure,
That is a memory, faded and unsure.

Yet sometimes a photo, a glimpse of the past,
Brings back the moments that didn't last.
You ponder the how, the when, the where,
And for a moment, you're transported there.

# 11. Time traveling chronicles

The adventures of a time traveler, bold and free,
A single step can alter history.
Each action a ripple, a world to reshape,
Past and future, a delicate landscape.

He dines with dinos, shakes hands with kings,
Paints with Da Vinci, learns ancient things.
Sees his own wedding, his parents' first dance,
In the realm of time, he takes every chance.

With creativity boundless, no end in sight,
He journeys through eras, day and night.
A time traveler, with stories untold,
In the tapestry of time, his adventures unfold.

# 12. The house of horrors

The enigma of a haunted house, old and grand,
A place where spirits linger, a spectral band.
Rusty and worn, it stands in decay,
A mansion where shadows come out to play.

Why dwell in darkness, seeking revenge,
When heaven's peace is within your range?
Chills down your spine, whispers in the night,
A haunted house, a place of fright.

Yet some choose to stay, bound by their past,
In a house where memories forever last.
But why seek vengeance, when peace is near,
In the afterlife's embrace, free from fear?

# 13. Windy whispers

A dark eerie night, chills down his spine,
The whispering wind, a sinister sign.
In the eerie garden, dead plants sway,
Every step forward, a whisper's dismay.

The wind speaks of life, then threats begin,
Screams of his family, a haunting din.
Forced to confront, he faces his dread,
Yet the wind's whispers fill him with dread.

It pounces, he wakes, safe from the unknown,
In the comfort of home, no longer alone.
A dark eerie night, a nightmare's flight,
Vanquished by dawn's reassuring light.

# 14. Wings of imagination

Butterflies that walk,
Humans that fly.
All in the mind
Of a free child.

His imagination runs wild,
Changing movies,
Or the world.
Adventures without reading,
The world in his hands.

Colors vivid,
Everything runs wild,
All in a child's mind.
He can be the best at anything,
If he wants.

He holds the key to his path,
And he will continue,
As long as he can.

# 15. Mystery of the abyss

The Unexplored Ocean
What lies in the middle of nowhere,
The unexplored ocean.
We can't reach it, despite our efforts.

Unspeakable horrors,
Or world-changing discoveries.
What lies beneath the surface,
A place out of reach,
Beyond teaching.

There could be nothing,
No one to save you,
No man's land.
Why come here?
To explore and discover.

I hope we solve our doubts,
And find an answer.

# 16. Threads Of Friendship

The bond of friendship,
Knowing you like no other,
Like a brother,
Helping like no one else.

They are there, and so are you.
The bond you make is a memory.
A true friend,
One who speaks a million words with a gaze,
Or just talks.

Anything can be done.
You and your bestie,
Having fun.
That is the time of your life,
Bringing the most memories.
Enjoy it while you can.

# 17. Echoes of words

Words are powerful.
They can make or break your day.
They can shoot like bullets,
Or rush your dopamine.

Words are dangerous.
Insults can ruin ambitions,
Rude people can break your heart.
Some need only words,
Not weapons.

Be careful,
You never know when words strike a wrong chord.

# 18. Posidon's Realm

The world beneath the sea,
A place unknown to man.
Poseidon's home.

Those who live there are like humans,
Yet they do what we can't.
They have gills and a functioning civilization.
A land of gods,Safe from commercialization.

A land under the sea,
Beyond our minds,
Safe from industrial giants.

# 19. Echoes of a fallen empire

A Lost Kingdom
A sword stabbed,
Many killed in this fight.

There lay the kingdom,
Bare land.
From a great civilization,
Fortified walls,
A grand palace now rubble.
A lost kingdom,
Lost in war.

All those people now dead.
A great kingdom fallen.
The mighty ruler dead,
The monarch buried.
A no man's land,Now a flat piece of land.

# 20. Neon Lights and silent streets

A city at night,
Crowded stalls everywhere,
The rush of neon lights,
People grabbing quick bites.

The city is alive,
Everyone is free.
Some are asleep,
Others wide awake.

Party animals fill the spots,
Bargain hunters roam.
The city sleeps,
Yet some remain awake.
Many are out,
Many at home.
Silence and commotion,
All in the city.

The fun has just begun for some,
For others, it has ended.
Some play video games,
Others enjoy the night.
Soon, even the city falls asleep.

# 21. Rustling of the pages

The pages rustling,
That's the only noise you'll hear in a library.
You can turn pages with glee.

A nosy lady to tell you to stay quiet.
You can read delightfully,
And even take it home to continue your journey.

You can ride a cruise or climb mount everest.
Kill voldermort or see as they kill Caesar.
That is the effect of silence.
You just pull a book and read.

It's that easy.
You can savor a hot cup of tea in Italy,
Or pull a quick one on a criminal.